RAGNAR LOTHBROK

The Incredible Story of The Viking King

THE HISTORY HOUR

HISTORY

CONTENTS

❧ I ❧

INTRODUCTION

❦

Many believe that Ragnar Lothbrok (in some cases called Ragnar Lodbrok) was a Viking who rose to prominence and had great influence during the Viking Age (800-1066 AD). The exact history of his life and actions are somewhat unclear as they are mixed with legend and lore. He was almost certainly a King with power over a group of people. He was also reportedly a strong warrior of great aspirations that may have raided Ireland in the earliest years of the Viking period.

❦

Ancient Norse sagas and various Latin historical chronicles describe Viking raids that befell Ireland from 832-845. Saxo Grammaticus, a Christian Dane historian, believes that it was

Ragnar Lothbrok who planned and executed the invasions of Ireland. However, two more modern historians, John O'Donovan and Charles Haliday, disagree with that assessment. They believe that it was another Viking, Turgesius, who may have led raids on Ireland in 837, and not Ragnar Lothbrok.

࿇

In some cases, such as this one, historians and historical accounts are not quite sure who Ragnar Lothbrock truly was or even if he was actually a real person. He could have been one extraordinary man, whose true actions were perhaps sensationalized over time. The tales of Ragnar Lothbrok could also simply be entwined with a combination of stories from other legendary men. Alternatively, Ragnar Lothbrock could be nothing more than a creative amalgamation of other known people, including: King Horik I, King Reginfrid, Reginherus (who reportedly besieged Paris in 845), and Ragnall (a warrior of the Irish Annals).

࿇

As a reader, you may wonder how it can be that historians are not certain about who Ragnar was or if he even truly existed. This historical confusion is due to the complicated nature of history, along with the lack of accurate historical record. The time period in which Ragnar Lothbrok reportedly lived is not well-known for its record keeping. Many people were illiterate and could not write down or record historical facts. People were also most often just focused on survival rather than record keeping. History was conveyed through stories, which could be fictionalized for entertainment. Over-time, facts were simply lost or re-written (for example, people cannot even agree on the spelling of his name)

⚜

Historical researchers do attempt to examine the past to uncover the truth. However, the source records are unclear. The information recorded may not be clearly written (sometimes literally and sometimes figuratively). Some source records contradict with each other. The records are not necessarily dated well. Sometimes it is hard to find other information that could verify the records. Historians can make varying conclusions from those records. With the varied records, historians also draw conclusions that contradict with those drawn by other historians. Nonetheless, those conclusions also become part of the story

⚜

To develop this book, records were drawn from a number of sources: the Irish Annals, the Orkney Saga, various Norse Sagas, the Saga of Harald Fairhair, various Icelandic Sagas, the *Gesta Danorum*, and others. More modern recounts and retellings of Ragnar Lothbrok's history were also considered. You can view a list of sources for additional reading, at the end of the book.

⚜

Given questions around historical accuracy, this book will examine the legend of Ragnar Lothbrok through three lenses. One will be on Ragnar the man, which will include a recounting of his family line and basic life history. These are the best-known facts that historians believe are most likely to be true. A second lens will be on Ragnar the myth, which will recount some of his greatest conquests and accomplishments, including those that modern analysis suggests may not be entirely true (or may be attributed to other men). The third lens will be on Ragnar the legend, which will recount his progeny (and their own victories), the final years of his life, and the legacy he left behind.

❧ II ❧
THE MAN

❦

"Power is dangerous. It corrupts the best and attracts the worst. Power is only given to those who are prepared to lower themselves to pick it up."
Ragnar Lothbrok

❦

When you examine the life of any man, it is most helpful to start at the beginning. Like many great warriors and kings, in the case of Ragnar Lothbrok, his true beginning comes even before his birth. His family history and lineage must be known to truly understand his character and motivations.

RAGNAR'S PATERNAL ROOTS

❦

In Ragnar's time, fame and fortune, pride and shame, status and power, all followed the paternal line. Ragnar Lothbrok is the son of Sigurd Hring, a great king and warrior in his own right. Hring was the link in a family line that reigned over various parts of Scandinavia, with the degree of ownership changing as the result of battles for power. Sigurd's initial access to power followed his fathers, just as Ragnar's power followed Sigurd's. Though each man also had his own accomplishments that strengthened and extended the reach of their reign.

❦

SOME HISTORICAL RECORDS refer to a specific saga that would fully retell the life of Sigurd Hring. Unfortunately, that saga appears to have been lost to the ravages of time. Sigurd Hring is most notably known for being the father of Ragnar Lothbrok and for winning the Battle of the Bravellir against

Harold Wartooth (the reported King of Sweden, Denmark, and Norway).

⚜

SEVERAL RECORDS, known as sagas, provide information on Sigurd Hring. However, like reports on Ragnar Lothbrok, many of those reports are contradictory. Three will be examined here, to provide more context about the man that bred and raised Ragnar Lothbrok. These three are: the Hervarar Saga, the Skjoldunga Saga, and Grammaticus's Gesta Danorum.

⚜

THE HERVARAR SAGA informs historians that when King Valdar (great-grandfather of Ragnar) died, his son Randver (grandfather of Ragnar) became the King of Sweden. Meanwhile Harold Wartooth was appointed the King of Denmark. Harold Wartooth then extended his reach by conquering all of his grandfather's (Ivar Vidfamne) territory. After Randver's death, his son Sigurd Hring became the King of Sweden, presumably as the subking of Harold. Sigurd and Harold fought the Battle of the Bravellir on the plains of Ostergotland where Harold and many of his men died. This gave Sigurd the lands owned by Harold. Sigurd then ruled Sweden and Denmark until his death. At that time, he was succeeded by his son Ragnar Lothbrok. Harold Wartooth's own son Eysteinn Beli ruled Sweden as a jarl (under Ragnar's command) until he was later killed by Ragnar's sons.

⚜

THE GESTA DANORUM, by Saxo Grammaticus, confirms this

story and adds to it with more context about family lines. According to that text, Sigurd Hring was the son of the Danish King Randver and the maternal nephew of the Danish King Harold Wartooth. This text confirms that Sigurd fought against Harold Wartooth in the Battle of the Bravellir and thus became the king of Denmark.

⚜

THE SKJOLDUNGA SAGA informs historians of Sigurd's personal life. This saga indicates that Sigurd was married to Alfhild (the daughter of King Alf of Alfheim, and mother to Ragnar Lothbrok). Unfortunately, Alfhild died shortly after Ragnar was born. Sigurd later attempted to remarry, but it did not work out. Sigurd was an old man and he went to Skiringssal to take part in the great blots. There, he spotted a very beautiful girl named Alfsol (she was the daughter of King Alf of Vendel). The girl's two brothers refused to allow Sigurd to marry her. Sigurd fought with the brothers and killed them. Unfortunately, Alfsol had been given poison by her brothers so that Sigurd could never have her. When her corpse was carried to Sigurd, he went aboard a large ship, where he placed her along with her brothers. Then, he steered the ship with full sails out onto the sea, as the ship burnt. This story accounts for Sigurd's death, which occurred on the ship.

RAGNAR'S LIFE AND LOVES

༺❋༻

As noted, Ragnar was the son of Sigurd Hring and Alfhild. Historians know that Ragnar's mother died shortly after his birth, but little else is known of his early life or childhood. Of course, there are no school records to look back on and it is highly doubtful that Ragnar had much in the way of formal education. His history becomes more apparent as he entered adulthood and started to forge his own path. This path included multiple marriages following a divorce from his first wife and the early death of his second wife. Ragnar's third wife outlived him.

༺❋༻

As noted, Ragnar Lothbrok was married three times throughout his life. This was not unusual at the time as illness and childbirth often led to early deaths for women. His first marriage was to a shieldmaiden named Lagertha. His second was with a Swedish Princess named either Thora or Pora

Borgarhjort. Then finally, he wed Princess Aslaug (or Kraka, as she is named in some texts).

❧

RAGNAR MET Lagertha while attempting to capture Norway back from King Fro of Sweden. Fro murdered King Siward of Norway (who was Ragnar's grandfather), during an invasion. Fro then captured the women of King Siward's family along with various other women, who were living in Siward's court. One of these women was Lagertha, who was captured and taken to a brothel so that her captures could subject her to humiliation. When Ragnar came to rescue the women, they fought bravely alongside him. Ragnar was able to avenge his grandfather's death and retake the lands from the invaders.

❧

IT WAS ALSO during this rescue mission that Ragnar met Lagertha, who was described as a

> *"woman with the courage of a man who fought fearlessly"*

(in the text, *Gesta Danorum*). Lagertha's bravery so impressed Ragnar that he decided to marry her. However, entry into marriage was not so simple in those days. Historical recounts indicate that Ragnar had to kill both a hound and a bear, which were protecting Lagertha's house, in order to successfully woo her. After Ragnar's success against these animal guards, the two did marry. Records also indicate that Lagertha eventually gave birth to several of Ragnar's children: Eric, Agnar, Rognvald, Fridleif Ragnarsson, and two unnamed daughters.

፝፝፝

THORA BORGARHJORT (sometimes called Þora in the records) was the daughter of Herrod, the Earl of Gautland. Historical records indicate that Thora had two sons: Erik and Agnar. After her untimely death from illness, Ragnar, deep in mourning, went on a spree of violent and hazardous raids. Later, his sons, Erik and Agnar, died in a battle against Eysteinn Beli (a King of Sweden).

፝፝፝

RAGNAR DID NOT MOURN the death of Thora forever. One summer when Ragnar was in Spangereid, Norway, he had anchored offshore to spend the night. In the morning, he tasked his bakers to go ashore to bake bread for him. The bakers found a farm, where two people lived (Aki and Grima). These two had reportedly killed a King Heimir and had captured his foster daughter, Aslaug.

፝፝፝

ASLAUG WAS ACTUALLY the true daughter of Sigurd Fafnirs-bane. From a young age, however, Aslaug was raised by her foster father, King Heimir. Legend says that out of concern for her safety, Heimir made a harp large enough for Aslaug to hide within. On a lengthy trip, the pair stopped at Spangereid in Norway, where they met a pair of peasants (Aki and Grima). Aki thought the harp contained gold and gems, so he convinced his wife Grima to break it open. There, they discovered the young Aslaug. They then decided to kill King Heimir, as he slept, so they could raise this young girl as their own (they also renamed her Kraka). Even as a child, she was uncommonly beautiful, and to hide her beauty, Aki and

Grima constantly covered Aslaug in tar and dressed her in a long coat.

﹡

ASLAUG WAS of great help to Ragnar's bakers in their task. Later, Aslaud snuck away to bathe outside, something Grima had forbidden her to do, lest anyone see her remarkable beauty. Legend says that her hair was long, so long that it reached the ground when she stood. At the sight of her bathing, the bakers lost track of what they were doing and burnt the bread. Ragnar was upset at his burnt bread, but knowing that these were competent bakers, he set out to discover what had upset their progress. It was then that he himself discovered Aslaug and her great beauty. He ordered his men to bring her before him, but only if she had the shrewdness to fulfill his strange command:

﹡

Come neither alone nor in the company of another,
Come neither clothed nor naked,
Come neither hungry nor filled.

﹡

LEGEND SAYS Aslaug took but a moment to think and then complied with Ragnar's demand. She took off her clothing but draped herself with a net and wrapped herself with her hair; she took a nibble from an onion; and arrived accompanied by a hound. Ragnar was so struck with her beauty and intelligence that he wanted to carry her away and marry her immediately. She refused, saying that she would marry him when he returned from the expedition he was preparing.

RAGNAR AMID THE VIKING AGE

৩১৫৪

R agnar's life is about more than just good breeding and a series of marriages. His true power came alongside the rise of the Viking Age. The Viking Age is considered to have started with the sacking of Lindisfarne and concluded with the defeat of King Harold Godwinson of England at the Battle of Hastings in 1066.

৩১৫৪

As noted, the sacking of Lindisfarme is considered by many as the start of the Viking Age. This sacking was the result of history and factors that built over time. Situated on a small island to the northeast of Northumbria, the initial priory and monastery of Lindisfarne was founded in approximately the year 634 AD by Saint Aidan. In the century and a half after its founding, the site grew in prestige and position within the wider Northumbrian realm. In 684 AD, Saint Cuthbert was elected as Bishop of Hexham, but in a twist of royal politics, he swapped places with the Bishop of Lindisfarne (named Eata, who was the first native Northumbrian to hold the post of Bishop of Lindisfarne).

※

AT SOME POINT (possibly around the year 715 AD, although there is some debate about this), the Lindisfarne Gospels, which was an illustrated Latin copy of the Gospels of Matthew, Mark, Luke and John, was crafted by Eadfrith (who later became Bishop of Lindisfarne). The Gospels were richly illustrated. They were originally encased in a fine leather treasure-like binding covered with jewels and metals made by Billfrith the Anchorite. Records document that during the earliest Viking raids on Lindisfarne this beautiful jeweled cover was lost.

※

THE HISTORICAL DOCUMENTS, the Anglo-Saxon Chronicle details the event:

※

"In this year, fierce, foreboding omens came over the land of the Northumbrians, and the wretched people shook; there were excessive whirlwinds, lightning, and fiery dragons were seen flying in the sky. These signs were followed by great famine, and a little after those, that same year on 6th ides of January, the ravaging of wretched heathen men destroyed God's church at Lindisfarne."

ॐ

ALCUIN OF YORK, who was serving as a scholar in the court of Charlemagne, wrote:

ॐ

"Never before has such terror appeared in Britain as we have now suffered from a pagan race. The heathens poured out the blood of saints around the altar, and trampled on the bodies of saints in the temple of God, like dung in the streets."

ॐ

THIS MAKES Lindisfarme the earliest example of the damage and destruction the Vikings were willing to cause without regard for the history or holiness associated with any of the property they destroyed. Also, the triumph over Lindisfarme was the first documented and highly successful Viking raid, which marks it as the onset for the period of time known as the Viking age. In sum, as a result of the sacking of Lindisfarme, blood had been shed and gold had been stolen, and Europe was unprepared for the calamity about to befall it.

ॐ

RAGNAR LOTHBROK WAS POSITIONED to be at the forefront of that calamity. He had a historical lineage behind him. He had land behind him. People saw him as a legend and he had their support behind him. He was poised to become a great

Viking warrior and so he did. His life to that point had been marked by myth and legend and once he donned the robes of a Viking, it became even more so.

❧ III ❧
THE MYTH

❦

The world is changing and we must change with it.
    Ragnar Lothbrok

❦

When you examine the course and totality of Ragnar's life, nearly every point is touched by what seems to be details of mythical proportion. His forefathers, wives, and children each join into his story with their own mythical fantasies.

RAGNAR IS BORN OF STURDY STOCK

Various records indicate that Ragnar's father, Ragnar, and Ragnar's sons were large, muscular men. The records note that Ragnar's father, Sigurd was like his mother's people in stature and appearance (from the land of Alfar), which were larger, stronger, and more handsome than any other people in Scandinavia. Ragnar inherited these traits from his father. At a young age, Ragnar stood out among his peers for his strength and handsome appearance.

AS AN EXAMPLE of Ragnar's prowess, reports indicate that during a battle against King Aella (which Ragnar lost most due to his hubris), he charged into enemy infantry and practically tossed them about, even cleaving down several men down in a single swing. Was this even possible?

HISTORIANS THINK this could have possibly been true. It is possible that Ragnar and his family tended to be taller than average for the time, even possibly comparable to modern averages. This would have made a substantial size difference, if those around him were of average height and weight for that time.

❧

IN GENERAL, the Vikings were taller than other groups at that time. Archaeological records indicate that the average Viking man's height ranged from 5 feet 5 inches up to 5 feet 9 inches. In terms of variation, those living in Sweden and parts further North were taller than those living in Denmark, Frisia, Saxony, and Norway. By comparison, the shortest Viking was probably as tall as the tallest Anglo-Saxon living in England. Genetics and wealth, which allowed for a good diet could have allowed for a better physical state among Ragnar's family.

❧

HUMANS HAVE INDEED GROWN over time in height, weight, and muscle mass because of factors such as better food, better technology, better healthcare, and better genetics. This is due in part to better nutrition and a greater diversity of diets, as well as better medical care and the reduced risk of contracting serious diseases that would have greatly weakened or killed those of earlier eras (such as, dysentery, typhoid, typhus, tuberculosis, measles, plague, and smallpox).

❧

AS A MENTAL EXPERIMENT, suppose that Ragnar was 6 feet

tall (we have no physical record of this, but only subjective judgments of his size). That would put him between 3 and 7 inches taller than other Vikings. He would also be 7 inches to a whole foot taller than most Anglo-Saxon soldiers. While this height difference can be striking, the differences in weight are even more so.

◊҉◊

FURTHER SUPPOSE NOW, that due to the lack of easy transportation, machinery, and difficulties with long-term food storage, there would be a lot more physical burdens placed on people living in 850 AD than there are in the modern era. More physical burdens mean more muscle, more muscle means more body weight, more body weight means a higher BMI.

◊҉◊

THIS MAY NOT BE a perfect explanation, but if Ragnar, was as much as 6 feet tall, he likely could have weighed 177 pounds. An Anglo-Saxon, being just 5 feet 2 inches tall, would have to weigh 131 pounds to have approximately the same BMI as Ragnar. In terms of physical prowess, that is a difference of three weight classes in Olympic wrestling, which would not make for a fair fight.

◊҉◊

ADDITIONALLY, the greater muscle mass would have given Ragnar more strength. Moreover, Ragnar was an experienced fighter. He had already had ample opportunity to build up his physical might and war tactics up to that point. The stories may have been an exaggeration that Ragnar was crushing and tossing aside Aella's soldiers, but it is highly possible that the fight would not have been equally matched on a one-to-one level. This is a fine example of the line between fact and myth becoming blurred for tales of Ragnar.

❧❧❧

ASIDE FROM PHYSICAL ATTRIBUTES, history and legend also indicate that Ragnar had some pretty famous forefathers. Genealogical records tell of King Hroarr who ruled in Denmark in the early years of the 6th Century, along with his progeny. King Hroarr had a son named Valdar, who was the father of Harald the Old, who was the father of Halfdan the Valiant, who was the father of Ivar Vidfamne, who was the maternal grandfather of Harald Wartooth, who was the uncle of Sigurd Hring, who was the father of the incredible Viking Ragnar Lothbrok.

❧❧❧

KING HROARR probably does not stand out in the minds of many people. However, he also was referred to under a different name that may: Hrothgar. This is the same King Hrothgar that countless readers encounter in the epic tale of Beowulf. Moving forward, Ragnar is a link in a family line that continued to have famous figures. For example, genealogical records also tied the family line to the well-known, William the Conqueror, who became King of England.

LAGERTHA'S TORCH STILL
BURNS

᭡᭢᭡

When Ragnar courted his first wife Lagertha, he bravely fought a bear and a hound to win her heart. Yet, the battle left as many scars on his heart as it did his body. He resented her for hiding behind these barriers and making him work so very hard to win her hand in marriage. When he met Thora (his soon-to-be second wife) his eyes wandered and so did that wounded heart. He soon divorced Lagertha so that he could kindle a new love.

᭡᭢᭡

YET, Lagertha could not easily let go of her then unrequited flame for Ragnar. During a battle, Ragnar sought friendly assistance from Norway, by way of his then ex-wife, Lagertha. Although remarried by that time, her early love for Ragnar was still strong. She quickly set sail (along with her new husband and son) and offered one-hundred-and-twenty ships to Ragnar despite his having cast her aside with divorce, in favor of a new wife.

RECORDS SAY that during the battle, Lagertha had a brave spirit. Reportedly, she flew round to the rear of the enemy (indeed, legend says Lagertha could fly because her mother was a Valkyrie) and caught them off-guard. Later, when Lagertha had gone home after the battle, she murdered her second-husband. She then usurped his throne and his land. She had finally decided it would be more pleasant to rule without a husband than to share the throne with him.

RAGNAR DEFEATS THE LINNORM

❧

Ragnar's second wife, Thora, had a bit of myth and lore around her own life, which laid the foundation for some incredible tales about Ragnar himself. Legend has it that her father gave her a baby linnorm (a sort of Norse dragon) as a present. Reportedly, Thora kept the linnorm in a box, and it slept upon a bed of gold. As the monster grew, so did its bed of gold.

❧

EVENTUALLY, the linnorm grew so large that it could not be kept in the box. It, ultimately, grew so large that it could not even be kept in the house, and so it curled itself around the foundations of the family home. It also grew to be exceedingly violent and attacked most people who came near it. The linnorm was said to have consumed an entire ox each day.

❧

THORA'S FATHER, Herrod, grew quite afraid of the creature and promised his daughter's hand to any man with the courage and strength to kill it. Furthermore, he promised the linnorm's bed of gold as a dowry to any such man. Some time went by, but no one was willing to take on the challenge of the linnorm.

⚜

ACCORDING TO THE LEGEND, eventually, the heroic Ragnar appeared. In this epic tale, Ragnar was said to be a giant, stronger than five men, and dashingly attractive. The records also emphasize that Ragnar was the eldest son of King Sigurd, who was also known as being the biggest, strongest, and most attractive man alive during his own lifetime. Clearly, Ragnar was a prince among men and so fitting for the hand of the lovely, but guarded Thora.

⚜

THE LEGEND SAYS that when Ragnar learned of the Earl's offer for his daughter and the dowry, he gathered a group of men together and set out for Gautland. Ragnar equipped himself with a set of clothes comprised of a shaggy cloak and breeches, which had been boiled in tar and sand. It was these shaggy, boiled clothes that protected him during the fight with the great beast. The attire was capable of deflecting many of the linnorm's venomous bites. It was from these clothes that Ragnar earned his name, Lothbrok, which means "hairy-britches."

⚜

RAGNAR WAS EVENTUALLY able to kill the creature by driving a spear through it. Earl Herrod lived up to his promise. He gave his daughter, Thora, as a bride, to Ragnar along with a hefty amount of gold as her dowry.

ASLAUG'S BEGUILING WAYS

❧

Ragnar's third wife, Aslaug, also has her own mythos. As noted, she was only adopted by King Heimir and was not his biological daughter. Her biological father was actually Sigurd Fafnirsbane, so named because he was known as the slayer of the dragon Fafnir. Her mother was Brynhildr the Valkyrie (a powerful woman, similar to an angel), who was reportedly condemned to mortality by the Norse God Odin for opposing his choice of victor in a particular battle.

❧

GOING BACK FURTHER into Aslaug's legendary lineage, Sigurd Fafnirsbane was the son of Sigmund, who pulled the sword Gram from the Barnstokk. Sigmund was the son of Volsung, whose mother was pregnant with him for six years. Volsung was the son of Rerir, who was the King of the Huns. Rerir was the son of Sigi, who was in fact the son of Odin. This makes Aslaug, who was raised by thieves and murderers, the great-great-great-great-granddaughter of the God Odin.

◈

VARIOUS TALES DESCRIBE Aslaug as a volva, which is the term for a Viking shaman and sorcerer. Within Viking culture, volvas were held in great esteem and were believed to possess great powers, so much so that even Odin would occasionally consult with one regarding the future. However, the use of this kind of magic was considered taboo for men, as it was considered unmanly because it had strong connections to fertility rites and various sexual practices.

◈

JUST AFTER THEIR MARRIAGE, Ragnar violated a specific rule that Aslaug had laid out for him—once he returned from raiding in England, they were to wait three days before consummating the marriage. Ragnar was impatient, and thus his first son from Aslaug was cursed. His name was Ivar the Boneless.

◈

SOME OF WHAT we know about Ivar comes from documents written in Latin. This is also roughly six hundred years before the printing press was invented, meaning that documents needed to be copied by hand. Ivar's moniker - the Boneless - may have been a copy error. *Exos* is the Latin word for boneless, *exosus* is the Latin word for hated. It is entirely possible that Ivar the Boneless should have been known as Ivar the

Hated. However, various Norse sources also say that Ivar was crippled, could bend his arms and legs in odd directions, and possibly could not walk. Such a state would match the curse that Aslaug threatened.

༺༻

AFTER SEVERAL YEARS of marriage to Aslaug, Ragnar's eyes began to wander. On a visit with an underking of Sweden (whom Ragnar had appointed), Eysteinn Beli, Ragnar met his daughter, Ingeborg. Ingeborg was young and beautiful. Ragnar was interested in strengthening the relationship with Eysteinn. Ragnar was strongly considering a divorce from Aslaug and set himself back home to tell her of his decision. Legend says three birds raced ahead of Ragnar and informed Aslaug of his decision. She was quite furious that he would leave her for this minor, appointed noble's daughter. Once Ragnar arrived home, Aslaug was waiting for him and told him the story of her lineage (revealing her link to Odin).

༺༻

TO PROVE HER LINEAGE, Aslaug told Ragnar that the baby she now carried would be born with a sign in his eye. Some months later, Sigurd Snake-in-the-Eye was born, with his right eye bearing the mark of a snake devouring itself.

༺༻

AFTER THE BIRTH, Ragnar turned his mind around and sent word to Eysteinn that he would not be marrying his daughter after all. Eysteinn was furious and felt that Ragnar had broken an oath to marry Ingeborg. The two soon went to war.

32

During the war, some of Ragnar's children died. Although they were not her birth children, when Aslaug learned of this, she burned with a great rage and shed tears of boiling blood (again displaying her mythical heritage).

❧ IV ❧

THE LEGEND

❦

How the little piglets would grunt if they knew how the old boar suffered.
   Ragnar Lothbrok

❦

Although the tales of Ragnar sometimes reach mythical proportions, history does indicate he carried out some pretty legendary feats. His actions won big battles, changes the landscape of countries, and inspired people towards triumph. He also left behind sons and heirs who would carry on his legacy.

A BEAST ON THE BATTLEFIELD

❧

I n all the attacks that were reportedly coordinated by Ragnar Lothbrok, the invasion and siege of Paris during 845 AD was one of the greatest military feats he ever accomplished. It was a success that added to his legendary status.

❧

IN RAGNAR'S TIME, Paris was but a small city on an island in the middle of the Seine River. For at least four years, the Vikings, under a number of different leaders, were fond of raiding in the areas around Paris, but they had never tried to assault Paris directly or capture it. Under Ragnar's leadership, the Vikings finally and successfully attempted to go after this prized place.

❧

HISTORIANS BELIEVE Ragnar's strategies were so remarkable they were later copied by other Viking chieftains: Gaange Rolf (also called Rollo, the first Viking leader of Normandy), Sigfred, and Sinric. These three also later laid their own siege on Paris in 885 AD. One might wonder about Ragnar's motivations, his strategies, and how they were so much more successful than those that came before.

❧

TO UNDERSTAND Ragnar's reasons for sacking Paris, one must examine events that happened four years prior to Ragnar's success. In approximately 841 AD, Ragnar was awarded land in Turholt, Frisia, by King Charles the Bald (grandson of Charlemagne, King of West Francia—the areas now known as France). Unfortunately, Ragnar eventually lost the land as well as the favor of the King (historians believe this falling out of favor was due, in part, to the continued raids on the areas around Paris). In sum, the two men were at odds and this contributed to Ragnar's motivation to take on the challenge of seizing Paris.

❧

LEGEND SAYS that to lead the campaign towards success, Ragnar brought down from Denmark, a fleet of 120 ships carrying at least 5,000 men. His flotilla entered the Seine in March 845 AD and sailed up river towards their destination. At the time, Charles the Bald and was largely unprepared for Ragnar's wrath.

❧

WHEN RAGNAR'S Viking forces initially raided Rouen on

their way up the Seine, Charles the Bald did make an attempt to unsuccessfully slow or stop the progression of the Viking raiders. Records suggest Charles was particularly concerned about stopping the troops because he wanted to protect the royal Abbey of Saint-Denis (located between Rouen and Paris) from destruction. Accounts do not suggest he had any particular concern about Paris being attacked, perhaps his hubris led him to believe it was well-protected, well-fortified, and indestructible against the Viking troops.

৩৫৪৪

CHARLES THE BALD assembled an army which he divided into two parts, one for each side of the river. However, in this case, Charles's plan turned into divide and be conquered. Ragnar quickly and successfully attacked and defeated one of the smaller divisions of the Frankish army. He also took III of their men as prisoners and hanged them on an island on the Seine. This was done to honor the Norse god Odin, as well as to incite terror in the remaining Frankish forces.

৩৫৪৪

RAGNAR FORGED AHEAD through attack after attack and defensive fortification after defensive fortification, making his way through West Francia. Eventually, he reached Paris and reportedly developed his plan for capture. His plan boiled down to brute and overwhelming force. Ragnar's determination and the sheer size of his army allowed him to accomplish his goal. This took the city of Paris by surprise. Never before had such a large party of Vikings taken on one single target. The move not only defeated the Parisians, it inspired future warmongers to take the same approach of using size in number to defeat any fortification.

⚜

THE VIKINGS ARRIVED in Paris on Easter Sunday, at which time Ragnar personally entered the city and plundered it. Once in charge, the Viking army kept the city of Paris under siege. The Franks could not assemble any effective defense against the invaders. The Vikings withdrew from Paris only after being paid a ransom of 7,000 *livres* of silver and gold by Charles the Bald (this would amount to a weight of approximately 5,670 pounds of gold).

⚜

WHILE THE INVASION itself was an act of revenge, considering Ragnar's earlier loss of land to Charles the Bald, this substantial payment may have been regarded as some form of compensation to Ragnar. This was, in fact, the first of a total of thirteen payments of so-called Danegeld (the payment system established to protect against additional attack) to Viking raiders by the Franks. However, although he had agreed to withdraw from Paris, Ragnar still pillaged several sites along the coast during his return voyage, including the Abbey of Saint Bertin.

⚜

CHARLES THE BALD was criticized severely for granting the large ransom payment to the Vikings. However, he had other more critical issues to deal with at the same time. This included disputes with his brothers, regional revolts, disgruntled nobles, as well as pressure from abroad. Since the political climate meant that Charles would have trouble trusting his own counts to assemble and lead troops to defeat Ragnar's large militarily force, paying them off instead bought

Charles time, and possibly peace from further Viking raids—at least in the near future.

VIKINGS RETURNED AGAIN and again to Paris in the 860s to secure loot or ransom. However, in a turning point for the history of France, the city's walls held against the Vikings' greatest attacking force in the next great siege of Paris in 885 AD. Even though, as noted, those Viking leaders used the same tactics as Ragnar. It appears, those leaders simply could not carry out the same level of unprecedented success, without the strength (and perhaps personal motivation) that Ragnar Lothbrok had in 845 AD. His success could not be replicated.

LIKE FATHER, LIKE SONS

৩৯৩

R agnar's sons proved to be, in some ways, even more violent and destructive than their father. They certainly fought their own battles and lived life on their own terms. This occurred most famously in the military campaign against Eysteinn (under-king over Sweeden), after Ragnar's failed engagement.

৩৯৩

DURING RAGNAR'S battle with Eysteinn, Ragnar's sons, were summoned to the battle-lines. Agnar was killed and Erik was captured. Rather than owe his life to Eysteinn, Erik demanded that he pick the day and manner in which he would be killed. He therefore chose to be executed by being tossed onto a spear impaled in the earth, so that he would hang above the dead bodies of his compatriots.

৩৯৩

FURTHERMORE, the sons of Ragnar were afraid of the magic used by Eysteinn. He had a great and holy cow named Sibilja, who with flaming horns was always at the front of Eysteinn's armies. Her bellowing was said to cause such confusion amongst the foe that they would fight each other instead of Eysteinn's warriors.

RAGNAR'S SONS hesitated to fight until one day, young Sigurd, demanded the right to fight. Ivar the Boneless, though frail, felt great courage at this and marshalled ten ships filled with great warriors to take the fight to Eysteinn. The other brothers followed suit, Hvitserk and Bjorn Ironside gathered fourteen ships each

WHEN THE ARMIES met in battle, Ivar led the great host for his side and ordered his soldiers to make such a noise that the bellowing of the cow could not be heard. This was not effective as the cow's wails could echo off the trees and ground. Ivar needed a new plan. Being great with a bow and arrow, he shot out Sibilja's eyes. However, the cow still would not back down.

IVAR THEN DEMANDED that his men throw him onto the cow so that he could crush it. They did so, and Ivar landed with such force that the cow was nearly driven into the ground. Ivar then slashed at it with his axe to kill it. Once the cow was dead, Eysteinn's army was driven from the battlefield.

The sons, feeling their brothers avenged, saw to it that the Swedes were not pillaged afterwards.

❦

INSTEAD, the sons turned their attention south, pillaging and making war as they went. They destroyed the fortifications at Wifilisburg, and captured the port city of Luna, on the northern border of Tuscany (which is in northern Italy). At one point, the sons were debating a raid on Rome. However, when they reached Luna, the sons encountered an elderly man travelling with two pairs of iron boots.

❦

RAGNAR'S SONS inquired of this elderly man for an estimate of the distance to Rome. The man said that he had worn out two pairs of iron boots travelling there on foot from Luna. The sons, taking this travelling old man as a sign of warning from Odin, turned back for home. Once their raids were over, the sons returned to Denmark and divided the spoils amongst themselves.

PRIDE COMETH BEFORE
THE FALL

❦

The most well-recognized reports on the death of Ragnar Lothbrok present his demise as heroically legendary. Yet, his end may have come earlier than needed, as it was his own pride and jealousy that led to his downfall.

❦

WHILE RAGNAR'S sons were rampaging through what is now Germany and Northern Italy, he initially stayed at home. However, while waiting, he heard of the things his sons had done. Ragnar came to believe that his sons might reach the great city of Rome itself. He feared their successes might exceed his own. Ragnar was prideful and was not to be outdone by them.

❦

RAGNAR COMMISSIONED the building of two great sea vessels with which he would sail to England and conquer it. His third wife, Aslaug gave him counsel that this was a bad decision. She believed that his army should be split amongst several smaller ships. This could make the invasion easier and it could reduce the risk to Ragnar's troops (in case a ship should be lost in the voyage). Ragnar, caught up in his hubris and folly, did not listen to his wife. To compound his error, Ragnar only took with him 500 men to conquer England. He did, however, wear his tar-boiled and shaggy garments, along with a magical cloak given to him by his wife.

❦

DISASTER STRUCK AS THE 'FLEET' of just two ships reached England. A storm ravaged the ships and drove them aground onto English soil, which made any hope of retreat impossible. In addition, King Aella of Northumbria had received word that Ragnar had come to take his kingdom. Aella gathered together a great host to oppose Ragnar by conscripting every single able-bodied man who could either ride a horse or hold a shield. Aella was still afraid of Ragnar and his sons, and of the terror they could unleash upon him. Therefore, Aella ordered his men that if they were to find Ragnar, they were to not attack him. Aella feared that if an attack led to Ragnar's death, his sons might descend on Aella, the troops, and the country, to rain destruction upon them in revenge for their father's death.

❦

AS IT WAS, Ragnar had nothing but a few hundred men, his uniform of shaggy clothing, a helmet, and the great spear that he had once used to slay the linnorm (that was guarding

Thora's home). Once the battle began, Ragnar's much smaller army quickly began to disintegrate. Ragnar, though, was unafraid of the enemy and rushed at them several times. Legend says that Ragnar struck with such force that he would blow down several foes at once. It seemed that nothing could stand against his fury and nothing could quench his blood-lust. Nothing seemed to bring him down: arrows, spears, swords, or horse hooves.

⚜

AT THE END of the battle, once his entire army had fallen, Ragnar was surrounded and exhausted. Aella demanded to know who he was, but Ragnar gave no answer. Aella commanded that with no identity provided, this unknown man should be thrown into a large pit of venomous snakes. Aella said that if this man were to give any sign that he was Ragnar, that he would be let go.

⚜

RAGNAR WAS TOSSED into the pit, but legends says the vipers either could not or did not even attempt to bite him. Aella's men were troubled by this—first their weapons could not harm this man and now snakes could not either. Aella, after some time, instructed his men to pull their prisoner out of the pit, strip him naked, then put him back in the pit. Now that Ragnar did not have his tar-boiled clothing and magical cloak, the snakes made quick work of him. Various records suggest that Aella had no idea that it was Ragnar that he had thrown into the pit with the snakes. As he had suspected, Aella would soon come to regret this decision.

47

REVENGE IS A DISH BEST
SERVED THROUGH WAR

꧁꧂

I t is not certain how King Aella had learned that his dead prisoner was, indeed, Ragnar Lothbrok, However, the legend says that he did. Aella sent messengers to deliver word to Ragnar's sons. In an effort to try and prevent a coming disaster, Aella gave his messengers precise instructions to note how each of Ragnar's sons reacted to the death. Ragnar's sons (Ivar the Boneless, Hvitserk, Sigurd Snake-in-the-Eye, Bjorn Ironside, and Ubba) had returned from raiding and were back in Denmark, when they heard the news of their father's demise.

꧁꧂

THE LEGENDARY TALES say one set of messengers found Hvitserk and Sigurd playing chess. Reportedly, Hvitserk crushed a chess piece in his hand so that blood and fat oozed between his fingers. Meanwhile, Sigurd, who had been cleaning his nails with a dagger, cleaved into a finger so deeply that he exposed the bone. In his grief, Sigurd did not seem to notice the resulting blood or pain.

❧

ANOTHER SET of messengers found Bjorn working a metal spear. Upon receiving word of his father's death, he shook the spear with such force that it broke in two. The last messengers found Ivar holding court from the high seat. He changed color to a sickly pallor, but questioned the messengers regarding the fine details of his father's death and all the details of the battle beforehand. Once the couriers returned to Aella, the only one he feared was Ivar and not the others.

❧

AELLA'S PREDICTION was quite correct. Ragnar's sons were indeed wrathful, and sought cruel revenge for their father. Ivar, however, urged patience and did not outwardly show such bloodlust. Ivar appeared to attempt to resolve the discord by offering Aella the opportunity to make a *wergild* (payment of restitution) for the death. However, Ivar also had a forward-thinking plan that was quite cunning.

❧

THE EXISTENCE of such a payment was a longstanding tradition among all the broadly Germanic peoples: Danes, Franks, Angles, Saxons, Vandals, etc. Among some of those in English lands, free men would have a *wergild* of 200 shillings, a nobleman would fetch 1200, while a king would be valued at a total of 30,000 pieces of gold (half for the 'realm' and half for the king's family).

❦

IN SPITE of Ivar's protestations, his brothers raised an army intent on crushing Aella and his kingdom. Ivar departed from them, but without any contingent of soldiers nor did he intend to engage in any combat. His siblings' armies were defeated, and they fled back to Denmark. Ivar, instead, entreated with King Aella, seeking the payment of the *wergild*. Allegedly, since the brothers had taken up arms, they were not to be part of the payment, which would go to Ivar alone.

❦

IVAR ALSO REQUESTED an amount of land that he could cover with an ox's hide, which Aella thought was strange but let the request stand. Ivar then cut a hide into such a thin, circular strip that it could encircle a city. The records differ about what city this was, some suggest York while others say that it was London. Since Aella was King of Northumbria, it seems more likely that it would have been York. If so, Ivar then ruled over York and the surrounding area.

❦

IVAR TOOK this opportunity to acquaint himself with the local chiefs and nobles around him and turned them against Aella. Once he felt that he had acquired a large enough loyal force, he invited his brothers to invade again. Once they and their troops arrived, Ivar led the forces against Aella and the rest of the heptarchy (seven other small kingdoms that would comprise today's region known as England). Ivar's troops were known as the Great Heathen Army: a great force drawn from Denmark, Sweden, Norway, and Norse Frisia. Some sources suggest that it was the largest army seen since the times of the Roman Empire.

৩২৩

PRIOR TO THIS INVASION, most Viking incursions consisted of hit-and-run raids on centers of wealth, such as small cities or Christian sites. This, however, was different. The Vikings intended on gaining not just prestige and gold, but territory as well. The great invasion began in 865 AD in East Anglia, which made peace with the Viking horde by giving them gold and horses. The army turned north towards Aella's realm and had reached it by 866 AD. Eventually King Aella was surrounded, outnumbered, and seemingly captured by Ragnar's sons.

৩২৩

RECORDS DIFFER as to what happened to King Aella. One story about Ragnar's Sons claim that Aella was executed by way of a "blood eagle," which is a torturous method involving breaking the ribs out through someone's back and pulling out their lungs. This method is so named because when looking upon the condemned from the front, the finished product would appear as though he was a bloody bird in flight. This method of execution was considered a blood sacrifice to the Norse god Odin. Another text says Aella just fell in battle during 867 AD.

৩২৩

WHAT IS KNOWN for certain is that the Great Heathen Army

occupied York in late 866 AD and were attacked by the Northumbrians in 867 AD. The Northumbrians were, however, defeated, and they paid off the Vikings. The Vikings then set off for Nottingham and captured it also in late 867 AD. They then spent the winter, there in Nottingham. The Army then spent the next eleven years rampaging across England, going as far southwest as Exeter and north into Scotland.

❖

IVAR AND UBBA were in command of the Army in 869 AD when Ivar sent two of his half-brothers, Husto and Yngvar, to attack East Anglia. There, they captured King Edmund. Rather than forsake Christ, Edmund was beaten, shot with arrows, and beheaded, thus becoming King Edmund the Martyr. Ivar came to rule over East Anglia then as well. Ivar was then set to rule over parts of England as well as establish a great dynasty in the region of Ireland and the surrounding lands. Each of his brothers was also given land to rule and their reach extended.

❖

SIGURD MARRIED the daughter of King Aella, named Blaeja. Meanwhile, Sigurd reigned over Holland, Scania, Denmark, and Zealand. They had a son, Horda-Knut, who went on to become the King of Denmark. Bjorn Ironside reigned over Uppsala and parts of Sweden. Hvitserk reigned over in Wenland and Reidgotaland. Agdar reigned briefly over the Norway Uplands.

❖

THIS ALL CAME to pass because of Aella's poor judgment, and an action towards revenge, that ultimately led Ragnar's sons into even greater power.

BORROWED LIVES

❦

A t the outset of this book, it was posited that the reports of Ragnar's life may not be entirely true and may actually be the result of several lives having been combined into one. For example, it is believed that perhaps another Viking leader led the siege of Paris and that the tale was attributed to Ragnar Lothbrok, in order to bolster his legacy. To understand the possibility of this and to examine the veracity of the tales and myths around Ragnar's life, this section will present a few of these other legendary men, on whom the tales may have been based.

King Horik I

❦

HORIK I (DIED 854 AD) reigned as King of Denmark from 827 to 854. His reign was marked by Danish raids on the Carolingian Empire of Louis the Pious (son of Charlemagne).

It is said he rose to power, in part, by helping to assassinate his father (Gudfried), by expelling other rivals, and through other wartime actions.

❧

DURING HIS REIGN, Horik refused to convert to Christianity, as it was his enemies' religion, and he resisted attempts by Archbishop Anskar of Hamburg-Bremen to proselytize to the Danes. In 845 AD, Horik's army attacked Hamburg and destroyed St. Mary's Cathedral there. It was Horik's last major war effort. However, Danish raids continued. The Franks lacked an effective fleet, so the Danes were somewhat unopposed and unstoppable.

❧

KING HORIK SEEMS to have disapproved of these raids, for successful raiders constituted potential rivals. Occasionally, Horik even punished raiders. In 836 AD, Horik sent an emissary to then King Louis declaring that he had nothing to do with the raids on Frisia, and that he had executed those responsible. However, in 854 AD, King Horik I was killed by a nephew whom he had driven into exile (a nephew who had, in fact, become a successful raider).

❧

HORIK'S REIGN intersected with the time where Ragnar was most active in his own success. Although many Vikings had died in the plague during the siege of Paris, Ragnar lived to return home to King Horik. Legend says that while showing the gold and silver he had acquired to Horik and boasting about how easy he thought the conquest of Paris had been,

Ragnar collapsed crying. He relayed that the only resistance he had met was from plague and a long-deceased saint.

⚜

SOME OF RAGNAR and King Horik's actions and lives have been intertwined in the retellings. It is interesting that the two men were contemporaries and likely had some real-life interaction. However, it is Ragnar Lothbrok that remains more well-known and who receives the honor of attribution in the bulk of the retellings.

King Reginfrid

⚜

REGINFRID WAS a co-King of Denmark from 812 AD (when Hemming I died) to 813 AD (when he and his brothers were ousted by the sons of a previous king—Gudfred). He was probably a son of Halfdan (a Danish leader who became a vassal of Charlemagne in 807 AD). He was likely the brother of Anulo (died 812 AD), Hemming (died 837 AD), and Harald Klak (died 852 AD). He was probably also related to the Danish king he succeeded.

⚜

ON HEMMING'S death only Reginfrid and Harald were present in Denmark and they had to recall their brother Hemming from Francia. In 813 AD, the sons of Gudfred invaded the kingdom and drove out these three co-rulers. Only Reginfrid tried to regain the kingdom, but was killed in an attempted invasion in 814 AD.

THERE IS concern among historians that Ragnar and Reginfrid have been confused in the records, in part, due to the similarity in their names. This could have been mixed up during oral reports and in writing. It is easy to see why Ragnar has become more famous than Reginfrid, considering the comparative longevity of his success and the brevity of Reginfrid's reign.

Ragnall/Rognvald

ROGNVALD EYSTEINSSON, sometimes referred to as Ragnall, was the founding Jarl of More in Norway. There is also another Ragnall of the Irish annals who may or may not be the same person as Rognvald Eysteinsson. Records also indicate some historical lineage links may between Ragnall and Ragnar Lothbrok.

THERE IS no agreement in historical records on Rognvald's parentage. Records indicate he was married to Ragnhild, the daughter of Hrolfr Nose. Various sagas refer to him having six sons. The oldest, borne to him by concubines, were Hallad, Einarr, and Hrollaug. The latter were Ivar, Hrolfr, and Thorir the Silent. Hrolfr, was said to be larger than what a horse could carry.

ROGNVALD WAS MADE the Earl of More by Harald Fairhair. Records actually indicate that Rognvald helped to give Harald Fairhair his surname by cutting and dressing his hair, which had previously been uncut for ten years on account of his vow to never cut it, until he was ruler of all Norway.

⚜

ROGNVALD ALSO ACCOMPANIED the king on a great military expedition. First the islands of Shetland and Orkney were cleared of Vikings, who had been raiding Norway. The troops then continued on to Scotland, Ireland, and the Isle of Mann. During this campaign, Rognvald's son Ivar was killed and in compensation Rognvald was granted the lands of Orkney and Shetland.

⚜

RAGNAR AND ROGNVALD both had some great military successes. Each came from an honorable lineage. Each had sons who carried on a great family tradition. It is easy to see how the two might be confused in the history books, especially with the similarities in their names. Yet, historians work hard to identify and properly attribute to each man, the correct actions and successes.

Ragnall (of the Irish Annals)

⚜

RAGNALL UA IMAIR was a Viking warrior and leader who ruled most of Northumbria and the Isle of Mann in the first quarter of the 10th century. According to texts, Ragnall was the son of Halfdan, King of Lochlann. He was a grandson of Imar (this could have actually been Ivar the Boneless, the son of Ragnar Lothbrok).

❦

RAGNALL IS PRESUMED to have left Dublin with the rest of the ruling Vikings in 902 AD. It appears he settled and ruled in southern Scotland or the Isle of Mann, and some records have him as a King of Mann. He may or may not have ruled territory in western and northern Scotland including the Hebrides and Northern Isles. The earliest mention of him in the Irish Annals is in 914 AD, when he is described as defeating Bárid mac Oitir in a naval battle off the Isle of Man.

❦

IN 917 AD, Ragnall and Sitric, another grandson of Ímar, are described as leading their fleets to Ireland. Sitric sailed his fleet to Cenn Fuait in Leinster, and Ragnall sailed his fleet to Waterford. Niall Glundub, over-king of the Northern ui Neill saw these Vikings as a threat, and he marched an army south to defeat them. The Vikings fought and claimed victory. This victory was followed by another at the Battle of Confey, against Augaire mac Ailella.

❦

RAGNALL AND HIS KINSMAN, left Ireland in 918 AD to fight against Constantin son of Aed (the King of Scotland). The Battle of Corbridge was indecisive, but this appears to have been enough to allow Ragnall to establish himself as King at York. Ragnall moved quickly and soon imposed his authority on the Vikings there. However, his position as king of

Northumbria was soon challenged by a group of Christian Vikings who opposed his paganism.

❧

RAGNALL HAD three separate issues of coins produced while he ruled York, so he was quite famous in his own right. History records indicate it is possible that he was some part of Ragnar's family line. The actions and triumphs of the two could be confused given the similarities. Yet, Ragnar remains the more famous.

❧

These are just a few examples of the men and actions that may have been confused with, combined with, or developed into the tale of Ragnar Lothbrok. While these lives were lost to the ages Ragnar Lothbrok's life and tales became the archetype of the age. This may be because he appeared such an extraordinary legend. As did his family. As did the legacies he left behind. As were the lessons he provided to future generations.

❧

❦ V ❦

AFTERWORD

❦

Short of being able to time-travel and clearly see the past as it played out, it will never be known for sure if Ragnar Lothbrok was one great man or a compilation of many of his legendary contemporaries. Many records from the time were based on oral stories. Christian records of the time were prone to loss or destruction from wars and raids (Viking or otherwise). We can be certain that raids did occur, and Viking settlements were established across Europe. Several sources refer to a Viking leader named as Ragnar, Ragnall, or some other, similar spellings. Many other sources specifically state that the leader of some of the most legendary Vikings, was the legend himself Ragnar Lothbrok.

❦

No matter the historical truth, the stories we now know of Ragnar Lothbrok are those of a heroic and yet also flawed man. He showed that if one is tough, courageous, and ambitious, your life and legacy will live on long after you are gone. If you are really extraordinary, that life and legacy may even exceed what likely truly happened. However, his own jealousy and hubris led to his downfall.

☙❧

The arc of Ragnar's story is not entirely unique. He had a fabled and noble birth. He carried out heroic deeds and exploits. If the tales are to be believed, Ragnar was a glorious force of nature. He simultaneously defeated a hound and a bear. He slew a linnorm and gained its bed of gold. He married a descendant of Odin. He gave nightmares to those who would have otherwise felt safe. He stole from those who foolishly unguarded their riches. He bore sons who left France, England, and Ireland (and other regions around central Europe) quaking in fear. Those son's carried on Ragnar's legend. Historical records indicate that Ragnar's descendants or elements of his culture and history are on all sides of great historical conflicts and important historical moments long after his death.

☙❧

Yet, for all the romantic stories of Ragnar's defeats against beasts to win the fair maiden(s) (indeed, tales fit for a children's storybook or fairytale film), there is also so much evidence that says Ragnar was not a noble knight. Ragnar was and could still be considered a villain. By today's standards of behavior, he was vile and evil. Raiding was certainly not a leisurely or kindly activity. It involved killing, raping, torturing, and destroying of property. Ragnar desecrated holy and sacred places. Under the destructive cloud of the Viking Age, Christianity contracted, the Dark Ages descended, and Kingdoms shattered.

⚔

Simultaneously, Ragnar and his armies strengthened significant settlements in Normandy, England, and Ireland. They were even among the first Europeans to find American soil. Where there was vile darkness in Ragnar and the Viking horde, there was also a global force for change that we feel even today.

⚔

Further, although Ragnar's romantic actions have not yet earned him any children's storybooks or fairytale films, he does remain an iconic part of world history and even pop culture today. He is depicted in films and television shows that show his life and actions, both heroic and destructive. He became an icon. He achieved this status because he stands out as a legend among legends.

❧ VI ☙

RAGNAR'S LESSONS

What lessons can you learn from Ragnar Lothbrok's heroic actions and destructive ways to become a legend in your own life?

⚜

Overcome Obstacles

⚜

Today, most people living in westernized parts of the world, are used to a whole range of creature comforts (access to quality and varied food, free from a fear of global and deadly endemic diseases, and a general lack of imminent violence). It has not always been this way. Even in the very recent past, there were more often destructive wars that spanned the globe, which could touch uncomfortably close to home. For example, easily over 100 million people died in or because of armed conflicts in the 20thCentury. Further into the past, survival was even harder as dangerous people freely roamed the land bringing with them death and destruction. Every average day was also wrought with any range of challenges from access to clean water to how to gain food.

৩৫১

It used to be quite common for families, tribes, clans, and nations to use violence as the primary means of settling disputes. Likewise, death from disease was commonplace. A common concern for people used to be what to do with all the dead bodies. People used to live short, hungry, violent lives where women became deceased at the ripe old age of "died in Childbirth." Anyone was very likely to die from a horrible disease picked up because of an injury or contaminated water. There was no stable refrigeration, famines were common, painful and deadly diseases were everywhere, and if you had any money or property it would have been no surprise for it to have been violently stolen.

৩৫১

Yet, even with all of this death, disease, and destruction, some people lived. Some people even flourished. Kingdoms and Empires thrived. The culture did advance. For good and for ill, Ragnar Lothbrok was part of all of that: he rained down death and destruction, brought pride to the Viking lifestyle, established Kingdoms, and played a part in the developing cultures of Northern and Western Europe. All of this happened when Ragnar must have known that at any moment he could face his own death and destruction (if not from a fatal injury on the battlefield, from the waste thereafter, or just the challenges of everyday life).

☙❧

Ragnar could have died or been crippled in any number of ways: drowning, infected wound or internal injury, debilitating disease, having his throat slit in the middle of the night, or by being impaled upon the spear of a hated foe thereby ushering him off to Valhalla or Folkvangr (the Norse afterlives).

☙❧

Despite any related fear this knowledge might bring, Ragnar Lothbrok forged bravely ahead. He risked his life, against any obstacles, for his life and the lives of his people. In the end, even with his various mistakes and with being among the most volatile or even vile humans of his time (even leading to his own destruction), Ragnar did what he thought was necessary.

☙❧

Ragnar worked to overcome the obstacles of his life and times, to do what he felt was necessary for his family and people. Consider the way in which he would forge ahead during battle. Although, modern people may not need to forge ahead in battle, his bravery and perseverance past obstacles can be taken as valuable lessons to guide your life (along with some measure of gratitude that your own life is likely much easier than Ragnar Lothbrok's would have been).

☙❧

Put Your Family First

Although many of Ragnar's most victorious and heroic moments center around death and destruction, he was a person with average moments in his life, like any other person of the time. When not pillaging and raiding, Ragnar probably even acted in ways that one might find no fault with. On an off-day (when he was not pillaging and plundering), Ragnar may have even been a loving husband and an inspiring father. He may have even had close friends and comrades that he cared deeply for. Ragnar likely worked hard each day to improve the lot of his family and those around him. This likely drove many of his actions.

Given Ragnar's penchant for violence and possible motivations, several lines from another villainous character, Don Vito Corleone seem appropriate: "I work my whole life, I don't apologize, to take care of my family. 'Cause a man who doesn't spend time with his family can never be a real man."

Records indicate that Ragnar had some interest in family life. He was married to three different women in his life: Lagertha (whom he divorced), Thora Borgarhjotr (who died from illness), and Aslaug (who outlived Ragnar). You may wonder why he divorced Lagertha, if he was such a family man?

As a reminder, during courting, Lagertha was not immediately taken with Ragnar, instead she set a bear and a great hound against him. Ragnar killed the bear with a spear and strangled the hound. After this, Lagertha consented to be married. Ragnar was always upset about this, and when given the opportunity to marry Princess Thora of Sweden, he divorced Lagertha. In those days, that was a fairly humane approach (compared to more recent multiple-married figures such as Henry VIII, who had some of his wives beheaded to be rid of them). It seems perhaps, Ragnar was looking for some true love he could get from Thora. Also, remember that Lagertha still cared deeply for him even years after.

࿐

Another sign that Ragnar was a family man—he was beloved enough by his children that they each were deeply affected by his death (crushing chess pieces and breaking spears). In fact, the devotion of his sons drove them to violent revenge. They waged war in his honor and wrathfully avenged his death Ragnar's bloodline showed that when family is united, nothing is insurmountable.

࿐

Play to Your Strengths

࿐

Most of the time, Ragnar used his strengths towards success. Ragnar Lothbrok was noted to have been a great bear of a man, taller and stronger than many of those around him. Simultaneously, he possessed a keen wit and intellect, as shown in the odd instructions given to Aslaug. Historians can also derive from the various records that he was profoundly great at getting people to follow him, a keen sailor, a capable administrator and organizer, a just ruler, a courageous battle-field commander, and a brave warrior.

◈

As an example of his inspirational nature, Ragnar did leave his people with their bravery, and set of ethics. For example, he and his sons were responsible for spreading the notion of the *Althing* or *Thing* to England, an early type of representative or consultative body. Though this body certainly did not represent all of the people within a given area, it was a great leap ahead of the autocratic forms of governance in place throughout much of mainland Europe at the time.

◈

When these traits are taken altogether along with the time and place in which Ragnar lived, he was certainly born and bred to be a Viking King. He was not made to till the ground, fish with a net, or attempt farming. If living today, Ragnar would probably make for an excellent Marine or Special Operations commander, and perhaps eventually even an inspiring politician.

◈

This lesson from Ragnar—to use your strengths for success, is true for anyone. In order to grow, succeed, and change the world, you must play to your strengths. Do not too much energy on building up your weaknesses, for it may just be a waste of time compared to the good that you can much more easily accomplish by using what you are innately good at.

Simultaneously, merely knowing your faults does not necessarily produce life-changing accomplishment. You can also use your strengths to address any weaknesses without wasting time on them. You will not be great at everything, just be great at what you can.

❦

Stay steady at the helm

❦

Ragnar did everything that is listed above: he overcame great personal and mythical obstacles, he put his family first and he set a fine example for his children to follow (given the cultural context of the time), and he certainly played to his strengths as a ruler, commander, and warrior. However, the final lesson that we can draw from Ragnar's life, comes from his death. It is, to stay steady at the helm. One of Ragnar's greatest downfalls was not just his jealousy and his hubris, but also his inconsistency in his approach to similar situations.

❦

One way that Ragnar behaved inconsistently was by letting his pride and hubris dictate his actions. Usually Ragnar acted fairly intelligently, using some measure of caution and planning before going into a situation. For example, when he first encountered Aslaug, he gave her a test in the form of a word riddle before allowing himself to fall in love. He also made a plan before setting siege on Paris. Yet, when he learned his sons might overshadow him in their raids, he let his emotions lead him impulsively and recklessly into battle.

Another way that Ragnar behaved inconsistently, which led to his death, was that he did not use his own proven approach. Previously, he had successfully sieged Paris through sheer size and brute force. He used an unprecedented number of troops, at that time. However, when he went against King Aella, he chose to do so with just two ships and a relatively small number of troops. Perhaps, it was hubris again leading this decision—maybe he wanted to make another unprecedented move for greater glory. Nonetheless, at the core, he was again behaving inconsistently with his own prior successful actions.

The third way that Ragnar behaved inconsistently was through his unwillingness to heed Aslaug's advice about the battle. She advised him to take more, smaller ships instead of just two as well as many more troops. Perhaps Ragnar was thinking back to Charles the Bald's own mistakes in dividing the troops, when he made this decision. However, in the past, Ragnar had heeded Aslaug's advice (when he thought of divorcing her) and it worked out in his favor. This time he did not. It was a terribly erroneous choice because it led to his later entrapment with no means of escape, and eventually his death.

It is one thing to take pride in one's own value and accomplishments. Certainly, Ragnar had much to be proud of from his history on the battlefield. However, it is an entirely different thing to let that pride bloom into a character flaw. It can contribute to inconsistent and foolish actions, which in Ragnar's case led to his being in a pit of vipers. One might wonder also about his judgment in not revealing his identity to King Aella. It seems that lack of judgment on this also contributed to his untimely demise in a rather drawn out and tortured process.

৯৩৩

All accounts suggest that Ragnar was typically a forceful leader, using that force well to the benefit of his people. However, like all men (legends and myths aside), Ragnar was subject to his own wavering mind and emotions. This provides a valuable lesson: to stay consistent with successful actions, watch out for impulsivity that might lead actions astray, and heed the advice of others.

ADDITIONAL READING

❀

Consider these texts if you would like to read even more about Ragnar Lothbrok:

❀

Ragnar Lothbrok and a History of the Vikings: Viking Warriors including Rollo, Norsemen, Norse Mythology, Quests in America, England, France, Scotland, Ireland and Russia
By Noah Brown.

❀

The Legend of Ragnar Lothbrok: Viking King and Warrior
By Christopher Van Dyke.

❀

Ragnar Lothbrok: The Extraordinary Viking
By University Press Biographies.

YOUR FREE EBOOK!

As a way of saying thank you for reading our book, we're offering you a free copy of the below eBook.

Happy Reading!

Printed in Great Britain
by Amazon